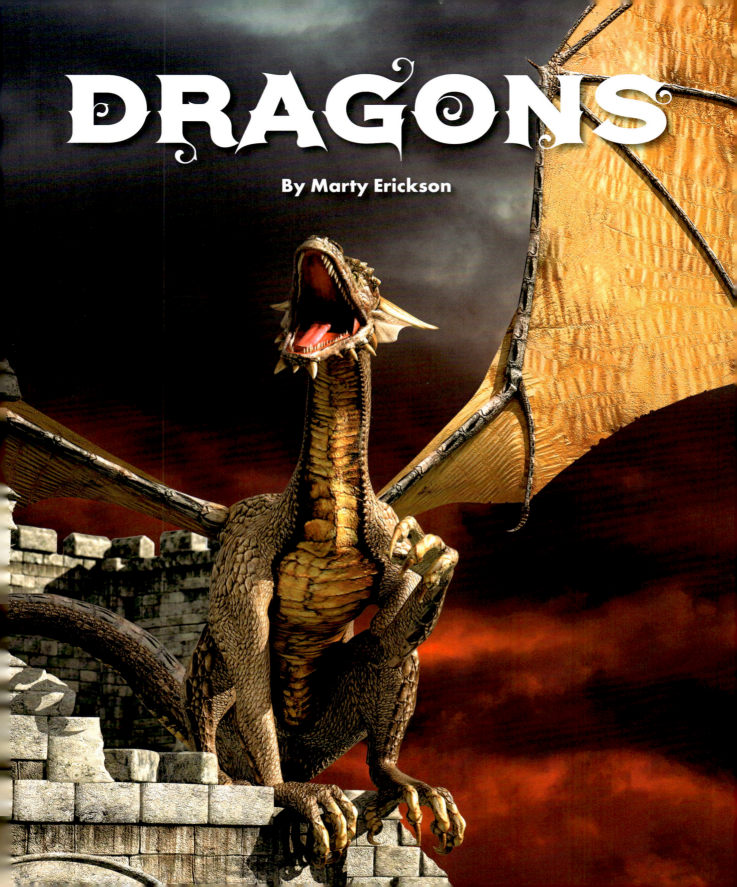

DRAGONS

By Marty Erickson

Published by The Child's World®
1980 Lookout Drive • Mankato, MN 56003-1705
800-599-READ • www.childsworld.com

Photographs ©: Shutterstock Images, cover (dragon and castle), cover (background), 1 (dragon and castle), 1–3 (background), 6, 7, 15 (top), 15 (bottom), 16, 18, 23, 24; Michael Gordon/Shutterstock Images, 5; Hoika Mikhail/Shutterstock Images, 9; Bill Perry/Shutterstock Images, 10; Triduza Studio/Shutterstock Images, 11; Chen Min Chun/Shutterstock Images, 12–13; R. M. Nunes/Shutterstock Images, 17; Craig Russell/Shutterstock Images, 19; Gudkov Andrey/Shutterstock Images, 20; Stephen Dalton/Science Source, 21

Copyright © 2022 by The Child's World®
All rights reserved. No part of this book may be reproduced or utilized in any form or by any means without written permission from the publisher.

ISBN 9781503849792 (Reinforced Library Binding)
ISBN 9781503850767 (Portable Document Format)
ISBN 9781503851528 (Online Multi-user eBook)
LCCN 2021939388

Printed in the United States of America

Table of **CONTENTS**

CHAPTER ONE

Cave Dweller...4

CHAPTER TWO

Flying Lizard...8

CHAPTER THREE

Scaly Beast...14

CHAPTER FOUR

Dragons in the World...18

Glossary...22

To Learn More...23

Index...24

CHAPTER ONE
CAVE DWELLER

A boy and his dad walk along the boardwalk in Yellowstone National Park. Steam rises up from the hot springs. Soon, they come to a pool of water. At the end of the pool is a gaping cave mouth. It looks like a dragon's mouth. Steam **billows** out. People are crowded on the boardwalk. They all want to get a picture of Dragon's Mouth Spring.

Dragon's Mouth makes a roaring sound. The sound comes from steam rising from deep beneath the surface. Bubbles of pressure pop at the roof of the cave. When the bubbles pop, a booming sound echoes out of the cave entrance. The boy smiles and points. He imagines a big dragon snoring.

The steam and sounds from Dragon's Mouth Spring in Yellowstone can make it seem like a dragon lives inside.

Many people visit Dragon's Mouth Spring in Yellowstone National Park.

All through the rest of their trip, the boy thinks about Dragon's Mouth. He knows dragons are not real. But seeing Dragon's Mouth has sparked his imagination. He wants to write stories about dragons. He feels **inspired** by his experience at Yellowstone.

Myths about dragons have existed for thousands of years. Many stories describe dragons similarly. But depending on the region, dragons may either be helpful or dangerous.

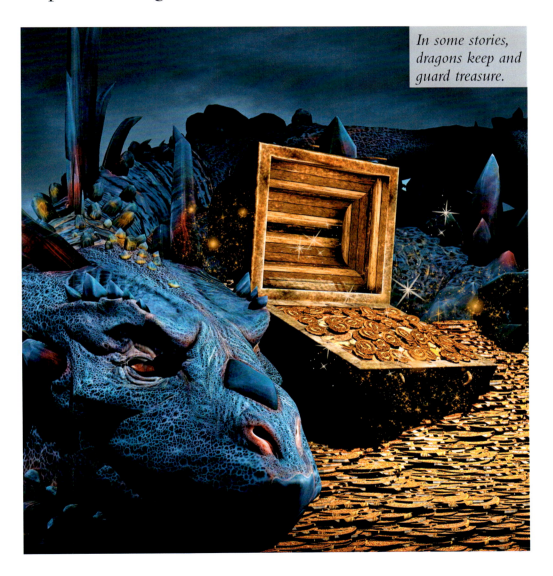

In some stories, dragons keep and guard treasure.

CHAPTER TWO

FLYING LIZARD

Early legends of dragons or snakelike monsters began thousands of years ago. Ancient Greeks used the word *drakon* to describe snakelike animals. Some stories from the Middle East also described evil snakes. Dragon stories existed in other parts of the world, too. **Scholars** think stories in Europe, China, Australia, and North and South America developed independently. Stories may have come from people seeing large animal bones or other reptiles.

Stories from ancient Greece and the Middle East featured large snakelike creatures.

One medieval dragon story is about Saint George. The story says he saved a princess from a dragon during his travels.

Over time, *drakon* turned into the English word *dragon*. Many stories said the creatures could breathe fire. These descriptions may have come from the Bible. This is the holy book of the Christian religion. The Book of Job describes a creature called Leviathan. It said this was a dragon-like creature. Leviathan had **scales** and breathed fire.

European myths were often influenced by the spread of Christianity. Dragons became a symbol of evil. They were described as fearsome. Only the strongest heroes could defeat them. Many stories about heroic knights fighting dragons appeared.

But not all legends about dragons describe them as evil. Chinese descriptions show dragons as kind and wise. Some Chinese art showing dragons is more than 5,000 years old.

Racing dragon boats is a common part of the Dragon Boat Festival. People say the team that wins the race will have good luck and happiness in the next year.

For thousands of years, dragons were used as a symbol of royalty. Dragons continue to be an important symbol in Chinese culture. Celebrations involving dragons include the Dragon Boat Festival.

CHAPTER THREE

SCALY BEAST

There are many stories about dragons around the world. There are some differences and some similarities. In most stories, dragons have hard scales. Scales protect dragons from getting injured. They may come in many different colors.

Dragons have sharp teeth and claws. They are **predators**. Stories say dragons catch animals such as sheep or whales. Most dragons have four legs. Some have two legs. They have a snakelike tail.

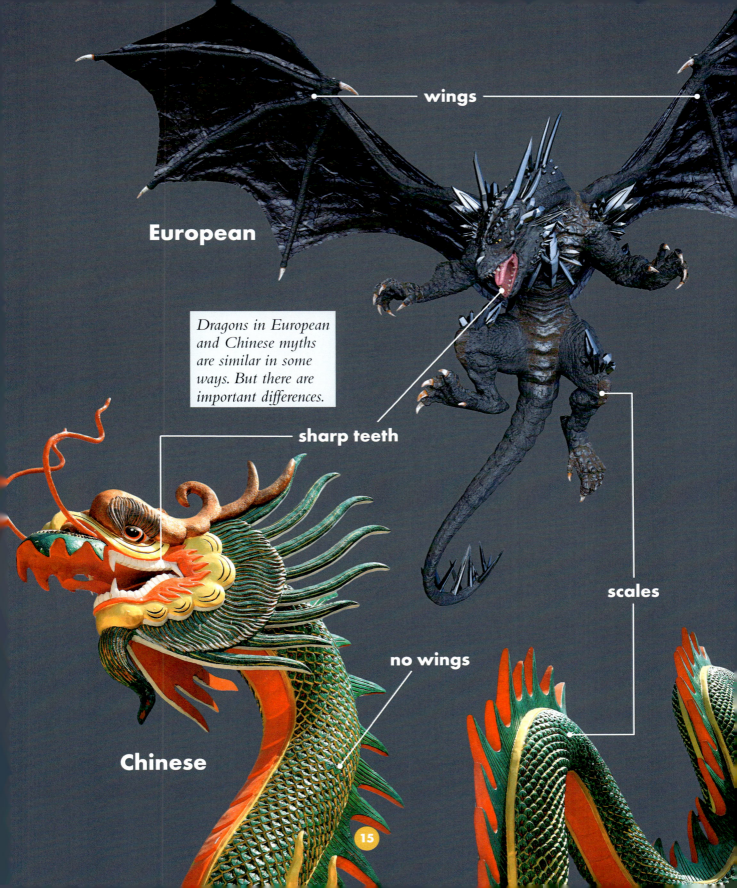

wings

European

Dragons in European and Chinese myths are similar in some ways. But there are important differences.

sharp teeth

scales

no wings

Chinese

Some legends say dragons can breathe fire. In European tales, dragons burn down villages. They attack people. These dragons are dangerous. Many stories talk about people fighting dragons.

Dragons from European stories are often destructive and dangerous.

The Wat Samphran temple is a Buddhist temple near Bangkok, Thailand. A dragon circles the 17-story temple. Visitors can step inside the dragon's hollow body.

Most stories say dragons can fly. But different regions have different stories for how dragons fly. European myths describe dragons with wings. The wings often look like bat wings. In other regions such as China, dragons do not have wings. Instead, dragons use magic to fly. These dragons protect the land and its people.

CHAPTER FOUR

DRAGONS IN THE WORLD

Myths about dragons may have been inspired by dinosaurs. When people first found dinosaur bones, they did not know what creature the bones belonged to. People did not know about the giant reptiles that lived millions of years ago. People may have created stories about a new creature.

Myths about dragons still inspire people. People continue to create stories about dragons. Many movies include dragons. Some movies are inspired by European dragon legends. *How to Train Your Dragon* and the *Harry Potter* series are two examples.

Sections of Universal Studios in Orlando, Florida, are dedicated to the Harry Potter series. Diagon Alley features a fire-breathing dragon from the movies.

Other stories use Chinese mythology. One example is the movie *Mulan*. The character Mushu is a dragon. Another movie with this legendary creature is called *Raya and the Last Dragon*. This movie's settings and characters are inspired by Southeast Asian culture. The dragon Sisu is a *Naga*, or water spirit.

Komodo dragons are large reptiles named after dragons. They are native to Indonesia.

There are no real fire-breathing dragons. But scientists and researchers named other animals after the legendary creature. For example, the Komodo dragon is the largest lizard in the world. Komodo dragons can reach 10 feet (3 m) long and weigh 300 pounds (135 kg). They have **venomous saliva**. A Komodo dragon's saliva allows it to kill large **prey**.

Another dragon-inspired lizard is the flying dragon. This is a type of gliding reptile. It has wing flaps. The flying dragon can spread these flaps and glide on the wind.

Dragons capture people's imaginations. They are not real creatures. But people keep dragons alive in the stories they tell.

There are nearly 30 species of flying dragons.

GLOSSARY

billows (BILL-ohz) When something billows, it expands outward. Steam billows from Dragon's Mouth Spring in Yellowstone.

inspired (in-SPIYRD) To have inspired something is to have influenced or brought about something else. Early discoveries of large animal bones may have inspired dragon stories.

predators (PRED-uh-turz) Predators are animals that hunt and eat other animals. In some stories, dragons are predators.

prey (PRAY) Prey are animals that get hunted or eaten by other animals. Dragons catch their prey with sharp teeth and claws.

saliva (suh-LYV-uh) Saliva is a substance created in the mouth that is sometimes called spit. A Komodo dragon's saliva contains venom.

scales (SKAYLZ) Scales are hard, overlapping plates that grow from a reptile's skin. Dragons have scales that protect them from injury.

scholars (SKAH-lurz) Scholars are people who have spent many years studying a subject. Scholars believe stories of dragons around the world developed independently.

venomous (VEN-uh-muss) Something that is venomous creates a poison that is dangerous to other creatures. Komodo dragons have venomous saliva.

TO LEARN MORE

In the Library

Alberti, Theresa Jarosz, and Sara Cucini. *Dragons*. New York, NY: AV2 by Weigl, 2020.

Marsico, Katie. *Beastly Monsters: From Dragons to Griffins*. Minneapolis, MN: Lerner, 2017.

Pope, Kristen. *On the Hunt with Komodo Dragons*. Mankato, MN: The Child's World, 2016.

On the Web

Visit our website for links about dragons:

childsworld.com/links

Note to Parents, Teachers, and Librarians: We routinely verify our Web links to make sure they are safe and active sites. So encourage your readers to check them out!

INDEX

Chinese dragons, 12–13, 14, 17, 19

dinosaurs, 18
Dragon Boat Festival, 13
Dragon's Mouth Spring, 4–6

European dragons, 8, 11, 14–17, 18

fire, 11, 16, 20
flying dragons (lizard), 21

Harry Potter, 18
How to Train Your Dragon, 18

Komodo dragons, 20

Mulan, 19

Raya and the Last Dragon, 19

scales, 11, 14

ABOUT THE AUTHOR

Marty Erickson is a writer living in Minnesota. They write books for young people full time and like to go hiking.